Presented with gratitude to

_____

from

_____

Date

_____

A Teacher Is a

Class Act

Compiled by Robert Bittner

Harold Shaw Publishers
Wheaton, Illinois

Edited by Elizabeth Cody Newenhuyse

Cover design by David LaPlaca

ISBN 0-87788-562-1

05   04   03   02   01   00   99   98

10   9   8   7   6   5   4   3   2   1

Contributors

Barbara Duffin currently teaches third grade. Over the course of her thirteen years as a teacher, she has taught grades K–6, both regular classes and special education.

Lois Dahlstrom has taught for eleven years in both public and private Christian schools. She currently teaches fifth grade at Faith Christian School in Geneva, Illinois.

Pam Hughes has taught behaviorally disordered grade school classes in Illinois, West Virginia, and Indiana.

LuAnn MacQueen has been teaching grades 9–12 in public schools for twenty years. She lives in south-central Michigan.

Claudia McBarron has been teaching for three years in a public school in Portland, Oregon.

Doug Stratton has taught grades 9–12 since 1982. He lives and teaches in Onalaska, Wisconsin.

Joan Weakly currently oversees special education for several small towns in southern Illinois. Previously she taught for about six years in a grade school in Centralia, Illinois.

"Students Respond" Contributors

Charles Moore was just "Chuck" when he had Miss Korns as a teacher at Patterson Township Elementary School in Beaver Falls, Pennsylvania.

Paul Oatman, now in college, served his detention at Charlotte Junior High in Charlotte, Michigan.

Thad Balivet learned his lesson from teacher Bill at Steller Alternative School in Anchorage, Alaska.

Julie Devine camped out with her teacher Mrs. Corkrey in Michigan.

Shari Martin learned journalism from Mrs. Rademacher at Pewamo-Westphalia High School in Pewamo, Michigan.

Elizabeth Johnson played hooky once—with her teacher Mr. Boteler's approval—at Sherwood High School in Sandy Spring, Maryland.

Krista Benson was inspired by her teacher Ms. Allen-Schmid at Flathead High School in Kalispell, Montana.

Compiler **Robert Bittner,** now a writer and editor living in the upper Midwest, performed his magic tricks and played the drums at Washington Irving Elementary School in Centralia, Illinois.

What's Inside

Introduction   9

1 At the End of My First Week . . .   11

2 My Greatest Satisfaction as a Teacher   15

   Students Respond: "Her Faith in Me Gave Me Faith in Myself"   20

3 The Biggest Challenge I've Faced   23

4 The Day I Laughed Most in the Classroom   32

   Students Respond: A Practical Joke—and a Life Lesson   39

5 My Most Memorable Student   41

6 The Best Thing a Student Could Do for Me   48

   Students Respond: An Unforgettable Teachable Moment   52

7 The Most Helpful Advice I Ever Received 54

Students Respond: One Teacher's Greatest Gift 57

8 What I'd Tell a New Teacher 59

Students Respond: A Guide and Support 64

9 Why I Love Teaching 66

Students Respond: Taking Social Studies to the Streets 71

10 The Person Who Inspired Me to Teach 73

Students Respond: Putting the World into Perspective 78

Introduction

Looking back, I have to wonder about some of the teachers I've had. Mrs. Schimpf, for example, let me bring my drum set and a record player to second grade and serenade the class (okay, the entire school) with my drummed accompaniment to old Beatles records. The records were loud, the drums were louder, and this was allowed to happen more than once. Imagine!

Or consider Mrs. Williams, my fourth-grade teacher. Sure, she encouraged my reading and gave me good grades. But what really won me over was the fact that she let me entertain our combined third and fourth grades with my father's magic tricks. In her classroom I was a star who squeezed blood from a stone, turned water into wine (it was actually a reddish concoction full of chemicals that came in bottles decorated with black skull-and-crossbones warnings), and made various other items smoke and explode.

By eighth grade, I would never have tried to impress my cynical peers with anything so childish as sleight of hand. We could still be wowed, though. We learned that the first day of class, when Mrs. Joan Weakly stepped through the door. First, we (at least, we boys) noticed that she was tall, brunette, and beautiful. As the school year progressed, we discovered she was also unusually honest and straightforward with us; in many ways she treated us as if we were already young men and women, instead of the awkward twelve- and thirteen-year-olds we really were.

You'll find Mrs. Weakly in this book, which is, in a sense, a thank-you note to her and to the thousands of other educators across the country. She and a number of other teachers share advice, encouragement, and stories from the front lines. You'll also find reflections from former students on favorite teachers.

So from those of us who have raised our hands in your classrooms, cleaned your erasers, set apples on your desks—and, sometimes, talked behind your backs and claimed the dog ate our homework—from all of us, know that you have our deepest appreciation.

Robert Bittner

At the End of My First Week . . .

I thought I had bitten off more than I could chew! I was not prepared for the children's energy level or for the variation in their abilities. I had several bilingual students, and that was a challenge in itself. Fortunately, I had two veteran teachers who were both helpful and encouraging to me.

—*LD*

 I said, "Wow, this is great!"

I took my first job teaching just one class of geometry and working the rest of the day as an assistant to the math department. I reported to work for the school year not expecting to teach and I was given the one class. I was so excited to be teaching at all.

At the same time, I'm sure I was overwhelmed. (It was a long time ago!)

—*LM*

The first two days went great. The kids were no doubt sizing me up, thinking, *We'll be nice the first couple of days.*

Our school had a policy then that all new teachers were to attend a day-long discipline seminar. Part of our assignment was to develop classroom discipline policies. After the seminar, I did just that, printing them up the next day on our ditto machine. (Does anyone still know what a ditto machine is?) All the time I was thinking, *My kids were so nice the first two days, I'm not really sure I need this.* After all, the policy was *very* assertive.

Boy, am I glad I had those handouts ready! Maybe spending Day Three with a sub had gotten their juices flowing. Whatever the cause, I walked into the room and could feel the tension in the air. I felt like a piece of raw hamburger in a room full of hungry lions. But, thankfully, I had my "double-barrel shotgun" behind my back: the discipline policy. I shot both loads and never looked back.

I was even smiling by Christmas.

—DS

The first week of school always seems longer than usual; however, *my* first week seemed more like a month. I thought June would never come. I wasn't sure of myself as a teacher, and I felt overwhelmed with the responsibility of being accountable for the education of thirty third-graders!

—BD

My Greatest Satisfaction as a Teacher

My greatest satisfaction comes from seeing the eyes of my students when they finally understand a difficult concept. When a student doesn't understand a concept I've introduced, it is my job and my challenge to reteach it so that he or she *can* understand. When understanding finally comes, it is reflected in the student's eyes. It is a wonderful thing to see and experience.

—*LM*

My greatest satisfaction as a teacher comes from seeing the appreciation and devotion in the eyes of my students. They truly do appreciate my work and love the attention I give them.

Each child is unique and wonderful in his or her own right. I love seeing them learn, succeed, grow, and become more confident.

—*JW*

It's very satisfying when students return from college and thank me for preparing them. I know that a lot of teachers of younger students may not always see the finished product like I do. I feel fortunate to be at the end of the spectrum, where I see the results of the influence of many, many teachers.

I walked into the local mall one day and felt that I was some important dignitary when two young ladies working at the cashier's counter began lavishing praises on me. They had taken both first- and second-year chemistry with me and had just finished their first semester of college chemistry. From the way they talked, I guess I must have done a good job in the classroom.

Moments like those are few and therefore very precious. Most students never get the chance or take the time to thank those who have helped them succeed in life. I'm thankful for the students who have taken the time to do that for me.

—DS

What satisfies me the most is seeing the results of my teaching, knowing I made a difference in a child's life. For instance, I had a student I'll call Gary whom I could only describe as obnoxious and obstinate. I thought I was being punished somehow when I ended up teaching him for both sixth and seventh grade.

But Gary surprised me. Much to my amazement, he changed when he realized I was truly trying to care for him, that I was trying to like him as a person. That revelation made a real difference in our relationship and for him as a person. After he graduated, I ran into him at a mall, and he called out to me. We chatted, and I was just floored, seeing how he remembered me and what I had meant to him.

—PH

I get the most satisfaction from watching the "light bulbs" come on and seeing the children becoming excited about something we're studying.

Currently I live and teach near the ocean, but the children aren't aware of ocean ecology. Taking them there to study animal and plant life, as well as the effects humans and weather have on the beach, opens their eyes to the fact that the beach means much more than just playing in the water.

We now have a saltwater aquarium in our classroom, which we fill with fish we catch, so it is a yearlong learning experience. When we go back to the ocean in the spring, the children are much more knowledgeable about and careful of the life around them.

—BD

"Her Faith in Me Gave Me Faith in Myself"

*L*ike singing the "Alphabet Song," I had heard it so many times that I had learned to recite it by heart: "Chuck, you're not working up to your potential. You can do better than this!"

From my perspective, my grades weren't really that bad. They were good *enough*. Was it really that important if an occasional D found its way onto my report card? It wasn't like my entire future was in jeopardy because I received a D in an elementary-level science course.

But when my fifth-grade teacher, Miss Korns, uttered that refrain, something seemed different. When she kept me after class one afternoon to share her concern, there were two things present in her appeal that I had never before experienced from a teacher: pain and faith. Instead of hurting me, she was actually hurting *for* me.

There was also something else in her appeal that was different. Miss Korns seemed to believe in me. She had faith in me, giving me faith in myself.

Something unusual happened following our conversation: I started to study science. By the time the next grading period came around, my science grade had improved from a D to a B. And my grades improved in practically every other class, as well.

Five years ago I received my doctor of divinity degree. As I accepted my diploma, I couldn't help but think of Miss Korns. It has been over thirty years since I've talked with her, but the insight and spirit she shared have lasted a lifetime.

—*Charles Moore*

It takes so little to make us glad,
Just a cheering clasp of a friendly hand,
Just a word from one who can understand;
And we finish the task we long had planned,
And we lose the doubt and the fear we had,
So little it takes to make us glad.

—Ida Goldsmith Morris, "Encouragement"

The Biggest Challenge
I've Faced

It's very challenging to keep up with the changes in society. Kids today experience so much more difficulty in maintaining a "normal" life that education has to adjust and adapt just to keep the kids interested.

We, as educators, have to be all things to all kids. We have to be educators of our subjects, substitute parents, disciplinarians, and much more.

The technology that kids are involved with today also has made a difference in education. We need to constantly expand our knowledge in areas that are new to us so that we can educate our students.

The shift in the family unit has placed more of the responsibility of teaching morality on educators, as well. For many students, school is the only safe place for them during the week. We must maintain this safety zone at all costs. It is the future of our society that is at risk if we don't rise to the challenge.

—LM

I had just agreed to take over for a teacher who had vacated his position at the end of the first semester. I soon found out that his geometry students had been taught by the "Mr. Smith says" method. (Mr. Smith, by the way, is not his real name.) As a science teacher in a math class, I was inclined to use the "Let's think this through" method, rather than have the students simply memorize patterns.

I also discovered that Mr. Smith worked all the homework problems on the board the following day, so few students tried hard to figure things out for themselves. (I also learned that he kept kids attentive primarily by drastically altering the room temperature. For example, if it was a typical Wisconsin January, he opened the windows!)

My methods, though, soon got me called into the principal's office. It seemed the whole class had marched into his office complaining about my teaching style. Since this was just my second year of teaching, the principal decided he would sit in on my class for two days. After his visits, he called me back to the office. "Doug," he said, "I can clearly see the problem here: You're requiring these kids to think!"

Hooray, I thought. *The battle is won!* Unfortunately, the principal wasn't the one I had to try to teach during the next few months.

—*DS*

 My biggest challenge is to not become discouraged during a difficult school year. Some classes are truly more difficult than others. But you know it is a *bad* school year when the D.A.R.E. (Drug Awareness Resistance Education) police officer refuses to come back to your class!

—*LD*

The biggest challenge I've faced has been individualizing my teaching for each and every child and having enough time and energy to give each the attention he or she needed and deserved. The more attention I have given them, the more they learned and succeeded.
Some needed an extraordinary amount of attention, usually because they weren't given enough at home. Sadly, every year there are more and more needs in the classroom because of lack of parental nurturing and care.

—*JW*

For me, the biggest challenge has been teaching junior-high kids with behavioral disorders. To give you an idea of the hurdles, I remember trying to teach a writing assignment, and the kids responded with a host of gross or unprintable answers. Another time, during the winter, all of the children had left their boots out in the hall while we were in the classroom; later, we found out that one of the students had urinated in all of them.

It was especially tough knowing how to reach these kids. Many of them weren't disciplined at home, and a lot of them had been labeled with various disorders that they tried their best to live up to. Their parents often didn't give them responsibilities at home, and few of those parents were trying to build bridges of communication with their children.

In my short time with them, I made it a point to offer love and discipline. The classroom was the only place they were likely to find either one.

—PH

The biggest challenge I've faced is handling the stress related to implementing new philosophies and curricula. In one recent year alone we were instructed to use a new reading series, a new social studies series, new science kits from the Smithsonian Institution, and a new writing program with our improved computer lab and classroom computers. We were also directed to implement a values program and continue writing new curriculum for our integrated language arts in theme immersion units— all while making sure the children meet or exceed expectations on the state assessments given in May.

None of this takes into consideration the many roles a teacher must assume daily in the classroom: counselor, parent, conflict resolver, nutritionist, nurse, positive role model, and parent to the children's parents—all while making the student feel good about him- or herself.

Teaching has become much more than simply imparting knowledge.

—BD

I believe in getting into hot water;
it keeps you clean.

—G. K. Chesterton

 Success is not measured by the heights one attains,
but by the obstacles one overcomes in the attainment.

—Booker T. Washington

 There are two ways of meeting difficulties:
you alter the difficulties, or you alter yourself to meet
them.

—Phyllis Bottome

Life affords no higher pleasure than that of surmounting difficulties, passing from one step of success to another, forming new wishes and seeing them gratified. Those who labor in any great or laudable undertaking have their fatigues first supported by hope and afterwards rewarded by joy.

—Samuel Johnson, adapted

The Day I Laughed
Most in the Classroom

The day I laughed most in the classroom was at myself.
I never was very alert first thing in the morning.
That, and the fact that I was always running late and
had a very dark bedroom, led to a fun day for the kids
and an embarrassing moment for me: I wore one black
pump and one dark navy pump. The kids, of course, noticed immediately and pointed out, not so subtly, my
mistake.

—*JW*

One day Marcus would not stop hitting the boy sitting
next to him. I told him if he didn't stop, he was not
going to be able to have a snack with everyone else.
When Marcus smacked the kid again, I yelled, "Marcus,
you just lost your cookie!" It was such a ridiculous
thing to shout out in the classroom, I just lost it!

—*PH*

I'm not sure it was the day I laughed *the most*, but it is definitely the most memorable.

It was in a second-hour geometry class during the 1993–94 school year. Four young men who were (and still are) good kids all sat together in the right front corner of the room. Earlier they had been talking about the stock car races they were involved in. While I was going over homework and answering questions, the four of them "started" their engines, "revved" their engines, and then the front two took off, racing their desks completely around the room and returning to their starting spots.

Somehow I made a few remarks, and class continued. But to this day when I see those boys, and I do see them occasionally, they mention that car race.

—*LM*

The day I laughed most in the fifth-grade classroom was when we were reviewing the process of writing research papers. After six weeks of work, I asked the class to fill out an evaluation of the process. The final question I asked was, "What grade do you deserve?" Rick, who was a slower student, wrote, "I deserve SIXTH GRADE!"

—LD

I have to admit that sometimes the most difficult situations produce the best stories.

My first year of teaching, during the second week of class, I decided to adjust the seating to separate some talkers. I tried to do it in a subtle way, so as not to draw attention to what I was doing. I kept the seating alphabetical, but I adjusted everyone one seat to "even up the rows," I explained. It worked. Then, a few days later, it happened.

I had managed to cleverly separate two talkative boys, one of whom was white, the other black. On this particular day, the white student was absent. As I was lecturing and walking about the room, I came up to the black student in order to ask him a question. Unfortunately, I called him by the white student's name. He was not pleased. He just looked up at me and said, "Boy, you're a far color off!" To which everyone else in the room responded, "Ooooooh!" in various ascending pitches.

The seconds seemed like hours as I struggled for a way to recover. It was going to be a very long first year if I didn't salvage the situation. By some divine providence, I said, "Yeah, but you both look so much alike!"

Silence. He didn't know what to think and neither did anyone else. Everyone waited for his reaction as I stood there with a smiling, apologetic look on my face. Finally, he couldn't stand it. My soft answer had turned away his wrath. He started cracking up, and the whole class followed.

I was saved! And, after that, he and I had a great relationship all year.

—DS

Cheerfulness in human relations is like oil in steel bearings: it reduces friction.

—George Landor Perin

 You spoke, one day, a cheering word,
And passed to other duties;
It warmed a heart, new promise stirred,
And painted a life with beauties.
And so for the word and its silent prayer
You'll reap a palm sometime, somewhere.

—Daniel Garnett Bickers, "A Little Kindness"

A Practical Joke—and a Life Lesson

avorite teachers make their impact as a result of a great sense of humor, good teaching methods, intense integrity, and a sense of fairness. All of these qualities were present in my favorite teacher, Mr. Duffey.

Every day, Mr. Duffey made me laugh as I learned. He made everyday tasks such as keeping a journal (which I thought meaningless and painfully unnecessary) seem important and worth doing. Previously I had done the work purely for the grade; now I did the work for myself. It made me feel good.

One particular instance, however, caused me to hate my favorite teacher. At least temporarily.

My friend and I were attempting to play a practical joke on Mr. Duffey. We locked ourselves in his closet and remained inside for the duration of the fifty-minute class period. That resulted in my first (and only) detention.

After class Mr. Duffey asked me how I felt about the detention. I realize now that he just wanted me to express some remorse over what I had done—in which case he would probably have torn up the detention. But, being both youthful and angry, I blew off the question and took my punishment.

A couple of weeks later, I realized the point of the detention: I loved having fun, but once "fun" became a disruption, it could be permitted no longer. Thanks to Mr. Duffey, the message finally sank in.

—Paul Oatman

*My Most
Memorable Student*

It was in the late 1980s and I was approached by a special education staff member who asked if I would be willing to work with Scot, a paraplegic with limited speech. Scot required an assistant for his daily routine. I'm always willing to work with the special education staff, so I said yes.

Scot is a special young man. In middle school, he was your average kid, with exceptional skills in hockey. But during that time he got very ill and was hospitalized with meningitis. While there, he was given penicillin. Through an error, he was then given a *second* dose. Scot was allergic to penicillin, and the second dose quickly put him into a coma. As a result, Scot suffered brain damage. He lost the ability to walk and talk, and he also lost most of the use of his arms.

Scot's brain was stopped at the age of twelve years or so, but he progressed enough to be able to attend high school and some regular education classes, including mine. The class was Math for Daily Living, and

Scot was able to learn to balance a checkbook, learn about taxes, investigate apartment living, and acquire many other daily skills. Because Scot could not talk, we communicated through a letter board and his signaling yes or no through arm motions.

This young man could do so much arithmetic in his head, so fast and accurately, that he amazes me even to this day. In addition, the other students were able to learn that special students are different, but are not to be ridiculed or avoided.

—LM

The student I remember most enjoyed science, and I ended up teaching him for six classes during his four years in high school. He was also my lab assistant for two years.

The combination of his personality, interests, goals, and character was a perfect match for us. I gave him the best I had for four years, and I had the chance to hear his appreciation for the effort.

I know that I don't have a great impact on all my students, but it is students like this one who remind me my effort is not in vain.

—*DS*

Fred was definitely my most memorable student. He had freckles and a constant, impish smile. It was like Norman Rockwell painted this child.

But Fred stole everything. I realized pretty quickly that I couldn't take my eyes off of him. If I looked down, he'd swipe somebody's pencil or notebook. It was so exhausting to teach him. He'd ask kids if he could put something in their locker for them, and then he'd hide it behind tiles in the boys' bathroom. When his hiding place was finally discovered, we found basketballs, backpacks—even kids' lunches.

—PH

My most memorable student was "Little Richard." He was a first-grade special education student of mine when I was teaching in a TAM classroom (Team Approach to Mastery, which had both special and regular ed students and two teachers). With twenty-five students, it took me a while to realize Richard was spending a lot of time in the bathroom. (I had learned the hard way that if he said he had to go, I had better let him.)

Once I investigated and talked to Richard about it, I discovered that was the only time he could be totally alone. He was the second child of six and was expected to take care of his four younger siblings at home. He even shared a bed with two or three others. With only one bathroom at home, and no lock, he said someone always was in there with him; at school, he could have the stall all to himself.

The problem was easily resolved: if Richard finished his morning work (which he previously had seldom done), he could take his lunch back to the classroom and read books while he ate. Once the agreement was made, Richard finished his work ninety-nine percent of the time. (A teacher would also stay in the room, working on the far side so as not to bother him.)

He became a different child, both academically and behaviorally. Richard taught me that you have to get to know the whole child and his environment in order to help him.

—BD

*The Best Thing
a Student Could
Do for Me*

The best thing a student could do for me is to take responsibility for his or her actions and learning. I can only do my best when students are willing to do theirs.

—*LM*

 The best thing a student could do for me is to be kind to others. Kindness is not cool in today's society, and TV does not portray it much. In the classroom, though, there are numerous opportunities to show kindness to peers. I try to model it, and I encourage the children to be kind to one another.

—*LD*

Sometimes I just appreciate the fact that they show up every day, pay attention, never have any makeup work to do, and usually have a smile on their face. The day-in, day-out attitude that says, "I'm glad to be here, and I'm glad you're my teacher" helps to carry me from day to day. I've also greatly appreciated the spontaneous notes and words of thanks I have received both from current and former students. (If they're written, I keep them in a special file to read on those especially hard days.)

—*DS*

 The best thing a student could do for me is to be successful and happy in school and in life.

—*JW*

Since I'm a Christian, the best thing a student could do for me is to share what they have learned in church with the rest of the class. It is difficult for such messages to come from the teacher, due to legal restraints. However, the children are welcome to discuss what they have learned in life and stories they have heard. The children who talk about what they learned in church on Sunday can help communicate messages of values, morals, and love for one another.

—BD

An Unforgettable Teachable Moment

One high school teacher who had a significant impact on me was a history teacher I had in ninth grade. His name was Bill. I don't remember his last name (it was an alternative high school in Alaska, and we went by first names).

Students were encouraged to take part in deciding how we would learn, and Bill had us discuss possible grading scales and then vote on our preference. The vote came out something like fifty-five percent to forty-five percent between the two grading scales. Naturally, Bill declared the fifty-five percent the winners.

After class, I went up to Bill and said, "You know, there are a lot of people that will be left out by this vote."

He smiled and said, "You're a very shrewd young man."

"Uh, thanks," I said. "What does 'shrewd' mean?"

"It means you're sharp—clever." He went on to talk about how a shrewd leader pays attention to the losers in an election as well as the winners. He made a lot out of that "teachable moment." And I lived for at least two weeks on his compliment.

—*Thad Balivet*

*The Most
Helpful Advice
I Ever Received*

You can't be all things to all students. You are who you are, and all you can do is your best.

—*LM*

 "Balance. Balance. Balance." (Thanks, Mr. Haraburda, for those wise words.) Avoid the extremes, consider your options, and, usually, the best road is somewhere in the middle.

—*DS*

 Get to know the student and fit the curriculum to the student, not the other way around. Throw out the textbook, if necessary, at least for some of the students. They all do not need to be doing the same things at the same time.

—*JW*

Laugh a lot—especially at yourself. It shows the children it's all right to make mistakes and that we can learn from them. By trying to see the humor in difficult situations, you can help lighten the stress level.

—BD

 The most helpful teaching advice I ever got was to pray for each of the students at their desk before the school year begins. During the year, I often return to their desks just to pray for them. This habit has changed my attitude in dealing with and interacting with the children.

—LD

One Teacher's Greatest Gift

*L*ucille Corkrey, my fourth-grade teacher, was nearing retirement, a time when many teachers would start to feel burned out. But she was one of the most enthusiastic, caring teachers I ever had.

Mrs. Corkrey took learning beyond textbooks—she took our whole class on a four-day trip to camp. We learned to cross-country ski, make crafts, name trees, and identify animal tracks in the snow. She opened up a new world by showing us how much there is to learn outside the classroom.

Her biggest gift to her students, though, was the personal attention she gave us. She had a talent for making each student feel cared for and special. That meant a lot to an insecure nine-year-old. More than the standard knowledge required of fourth-grade graduates, I gained more confidence in myself. Because she so clearly demonstrated that she valued me, I learned to value myself more.

The spelling words I mastered have been useful, I'm sure. But the other lessons Mrs. Corkrey taught provided a strong foundation for life.

—*Julie Devine*

What I'd Tell a
New Teacher

Relax. It seems as if there are a million things to learn at first. But that's what makes teaching a great career: if you could learn it all in a week, think how boring it would get after just a few years! I've been teaching for fifteen years and I haven't gotten bored yet.

The key is to focus on just a few things at a time. Start with things you feel confident about. As you get comfortable with them, move on to some areas that you're not quite so sure about.

Don't feel as if you have to give the highest possible quality instruction every second the students are in your room. Take the time to do your attendance, gather your thoughts and any materials, and begin. Don't be afraid to ask students to help with simple tasks.

You may not want to let your students know that you're a green, first-year teacher; they might turn into a group of hungry lions. But it might be wise to let your colleagues know. Ask for help and advice. Have big ears and a little mouth. Don't feel as if you have to be an expert on everything after the first week. It will probably take a few years before you really feel as though you have a handle on things. In fact, I don't know if any of us really feels as if we have it all figured out. I know I'm always learning new ways to do things.

—DS

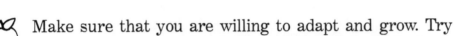

Make sure that you are willing to adapt and grow. Try your hardest not to become stagnant. Your students won't stay the same from year to year; why should you?

—LM

Have compassion for every child and realize the importance of what you do and say. A teacher's influence on a child's life is right up there with parental and peer influences, and a teacher's job should be viewed as extremely important in the life of her students. I have seen teachers who have made a very positive difference; I've also seen those who had a negative impact on their students.

Also, don't hold back the advanced students by making them repeat what they already know. And don't frustrate the weaker students by giving them work they can't possibly do.

—JW

 Love the kids and be consistent with your discipline. It doesn't matter how elaborate or simple the discipline approach is. The question is, Do you notice when they misbehave? Do you *care?*

—PH

I'd tell a new teacher to pray for each of the children in his or her class. Pray for their unique learning styles and their family situations. And ask God for the wisdom and understanding to know how best to help them.

—LD

 I would say "Relax." Don't just stand and lecture. Get to know and respect your children. You have to be the authority figure, but you don't have to be rigid. If you respect them, have a calm atmosphere in the classroom, interact with them, and let them help make decisions, they will respect you much more and be better students.

—BD

A Guide and Support

When I was in high school, I knew I could do well academically, but I didn't have enough confidence in myself. Fortunately, I had a very supportive teacher named Mrs. Carol Rademacher. She was my journalism teacher for two years. During my first year in the class (my junior year), she chose me as the features editor of the school newspaper. Although I was a shy and quiet student, she knew that I could write well and could handle the responsibilities of an editor. Throughout that year, she encouraged me to make the features section the best it could be. She listened to my ideas. She praised my writing. By the end of the year, I was feeling confident and able to handle anything.

At the start of my senior year, I felt honored when Mrs. Rademacher asked me to be the editor-in-chief of the newspaper. Although I was happy with my position, it was challenging at times. But again, Mrs. Rademacher was there to guide me, and I learned a lot from the experience. Then, as graduation approached and my worries about life after high school increased, I turned to Mrs. Rademacher for support. She was always there to listen to me. No matter how trivial my worries, she always offered an encouraging word. She told me that if I did as well in college as I did in high school, I would do just fine. With her rallying behind me, I felt assured that my future would turn out okay.

Although I didn't become a teacher like Mrs. Rademacher, as had been my goal for some time, I did go to college and did "turn out okay." I am grateful that I had someone like her who believed in me along the way.

—Shari Martin

Why I Love Teaching

Teaching high-school mathematics allows me to create in my students a *like* for mathematics. Of the many disciplines of education, mathematics is used so much in daily life that students need to feel that they are capable of doing it.

Many times my students hate math or feel that they aren't any good at it. Somewhere they have acquired these ideas, and I consider it a challenge to change their minds.

Teaching allows me to open windows of knowledge that might not otherwise be looked through by my students. It is my goal each year to create an atmosphere of openness in my classroom so that students won't be intimidated by mathematics. I want them to realize that mathematics can open many important doors for them in their future. There is no other job in mathematics that allows me to do all the things that I do each day in my classroom.

—LM

As trying as motherhood is at times, teaching is second only to mothering in giving back to me the greatest satisfaction and rewards. Each child is so unique, each situation at school calls for real professionalism, action, and insight.

There's rarely a dull moment. Every day teachers have to make decisions that could affect a child's self-image, demonstrate a life lesson, or merely let her know that she is important and that someone cares for her.

Children have unique views of things; they are perceptive, innocent, honest, and have an inner wisdom—traits that are often lost in adulthood. These aspects of children make them fun and interesting.

—LW

I love teaching because it gives me a chance to use the gifts and abilities that God has given me.

I always wanted to become a teacher, but felt it was an impossible dream. No one in my family had ever gone to college, and I had not taken the entrance exams during my senior year of high school.

One evening at a church picnic I met Dr. Richard Besançon, a professor at a new school called Judson College. Dr. Besançon asked me about my future plans, and I told him of my dream to become a teacher. He offered to take me to visit the school and check on a scholarship. To make a long story short, I enrolled and won the President's Scholarship. Three years later I graduated with high distinction and went on to graduate school at Northern Illinois University. I taught for three years in a public school, then stayed home to raise my family for eighteen years. Eight years ago I returned to my love of teaching at a private Christian school.

—LD

This is my third year of teaching first grade, and deep down I adore it. My students from last year all come down my hall and give me a great big hug at the end of the day. I also received a note on the last day of the first week from a student's parent: "Nathan says, 'This is the greatest teacher I've ever had,' and he's really looking forward to this year." I can go nine months on notes like those.

—CM

 I love people and I wanted to do something that would change the world. I haven't changed the world, but I do know I've made an impact on some people, and that's wonderful.

—PH

Taking Social Studies to the Streets

*M*y high school history and social studies teacher, Gene Boteler, gave me a great appreciation for history and a sense that today's current events are tomorrow's history. He encouraged me, and all his students, to take part in what was happening in the world and not merely to watch from the sidelines.

My fondest memory of Mr. Boteler is from my senior year of high school, after the American hostages in Iran were released from captivity. A big parade was scheduled to welcome the former hostages to Washington, D.C., about a thirty-minute trip from our high school in suburban Maryland. Mr. Boteler stood in front of our first-period class and told us, "If I didn't have to be here teaching, I'd be downtown to welcome the hostages home. I certainly wouldn't want to miss an important historic occasion like this." He then said he'd vouch for any student who felt the same way.

At least a dozen students, myself included, left the class and headed into Washington. Being part of the crowds cheering for the returned hostages was a thrilling lesson in twentieth-century history I could never have received in the classroom. The occasion was the only time I ever cut school, but it was also one of the most memorable lessons I ever learned.

—*Elizabeth Johnson*

*The Person Who
Inspired Me to Teach*

My mother inspired me to teach. She loved teaching and worked endless hours at home preparing for her classes. I was so proud of her. When I was in junior high, she taught in the same school. The other kids would always tell me that they hoped they would get my mom for a teacher, because she was the nicest and best teacher in the school.

That reputation didn't always work in her favor, though. I remember one particularly exasperating day for her when she had gone down to the principal's office to ask why he always gave her all the problem students. He told her that she was the most compassionate and caring teacher, and the problem students always fared best in her classroom. So much for the rewards of being a good teacher!

—*JW*

The person who inspired me to teach was Miss Viola Peterson. She was my American history teacher during my junior year of high school. She instilled a love of freedom and country through her story of America and its struggle for democracy.

I learned more than history facts from her, though. She saw the potential that I had and encouraged me to work hard. She taught me to be disciplined in my study and preparation for class.

I have carried these traits with me my entire life, and I now strive to help other boys and girls learn how to learn. I am truly thankful for "Miss Pete," as we called her. She gave me courage to try to do my best in all things.

—LD

I've wanted to teach for as along as I can remember. Engineering was an option I investigated in college, but education won out for many reasons. No one person influenced me to teach originally, but one person has influenced the *way* I teach.

My high school geometry teacher made my life miserable. I was intimidated, ridiculed, and embarrassed when I didn't understand something. That class has become my model: I do everything the opposite way. Never do I want a student in any of my classes to feel the way I felt as a high school sophomore.

—LM

Sue Donstad inspired me to teach when I was in junior high. She was the best teacher I ever had. At a time when I was not very interested in my parents' point of view, her influence was great.

She also led youth group activities at church. I don't think I would have gone into teaching with such enthusiasm—and I might not have developed such a strong faith—if it hadn't been for Sue's encouragement and support.

—PH

 My first-, second-, fourth-, and fifth-grade teachers inspired me to teach. They gave me fantastic models of teachers who truly cared.

—BD

Putting the World into Perspective

*L*ast year, I had a teacher who helped me not only to learn a subject, but to more clearly express my opinions. She even made me think about issues and sides of issues that I had never considered before.

Genia Allen-Schmid was my Global Village teacher last year. Ms. Allen-Schmid taught that class in a way that I have never been taught before: with student input. She actually asked us what we thought we should do and how we should do it. As the result of that approach, we really learned. By the end of the semester, I understood the idea of a "global community," global hunger, the United Nations, and even the war in Bosnia. Ms. Allen-Schmid not only taught us about these things, but always found a way to relate them to our lives, to put everything in perspective.

In Global Village, we had heated discussions almost every day (I believe our discussion on hunger and homelessness lasted almost a week). Because of this openness and encouragement of ideas, I learned about many issues that I was not clear about previously, and heard from people with very different ideas than mine. I learned more than just what was going on in the world: I learned why and how, and what other people thought of those events.

—*Krista Benson*

If you approach each person you meet in the spirit of adventure, you will find yourself endlessly fascinated by the new channels of thought and experience and personality that you encounter.

—Eleanor Roosevelt